THE BIG SHOW

BY ADAM STONE

TORQUE™

BELLWETHER MEDIA . MINNEAPOLIS, MN

Are you ready to take it to the extreme? Torque books thrust you into the action-packed world of sports, vehicles, mystery, and adventure. These books may include dirt, smoke, fire, and dangerous stunts. WARNING: read at your own risk.

Library of Congress Cataloging-in-Publication Data

Stone, Adam.
The Big Show / by Adam Stone.
p. cm. -- (Torque: pro wrestling champions)
Includes bibliographical references and index.
Summary: "Engaging images accompany information about The Big Show. The combination of high-interest subject matter and light text is intended for students in grades 3 through 7"--Provided by publisher.
ISBN 978-1-60014-634-3 (hardcover : alk. paper)
1. Big Show, 1972---Juvenile literature. 2. Wrestlers--United States--Biography--Juvenile literature. I. Title. II. Series.

GV1196.B57S86 2012
796.812092--dc22
[B] 2011006241

This edition first published in 2012 by Bellwether Media, Inc.

Printed in the United States of America, North Mankato, MN.

080111 1187

CONTENTS

SURVIVOR SERIES

The Big Show circled his opponent at the 2002 World Wrestling Entertainment (WWE) Survivor Series. This was the biggest match of his career. He was up against Brock Lesnar, his main **rival**. Lesnar was the current WWE Champion. He had never been pinned.

The two wrestlers stared each other down. The Big Show charged at Lesnar. He drove him into a corner and slammed him to the mat.

VITAL STATS

Wrestling Name: -------- The Big Show

Real Name: ---- Paul Donald Wight, Jr.

Height: ------------ 7 feet (2.1 meters)

Weight: --- 485 pounds (220 kilograms)

Started Wrestling: -------------- 1995

Finishing Move: ----------- Chokeslam

The Big Show stopped to show off for the crowd. Lesnar fought back. He threw The Big Show to the mat and hit him with a metal chair. Lesnar went for the pin, but the referee had been knocked out of the ring.

The Big Show got back up while Lesnar's back was turned. He picked up the metal chair and hit Lesnar with it. Then The Big Show used a **chokeslam** to throw Lesnar to the mat. The referee came back into the ring and counted to three. The Big Show was the new WWE Champion!

WHO IS THE BIG SHOW?

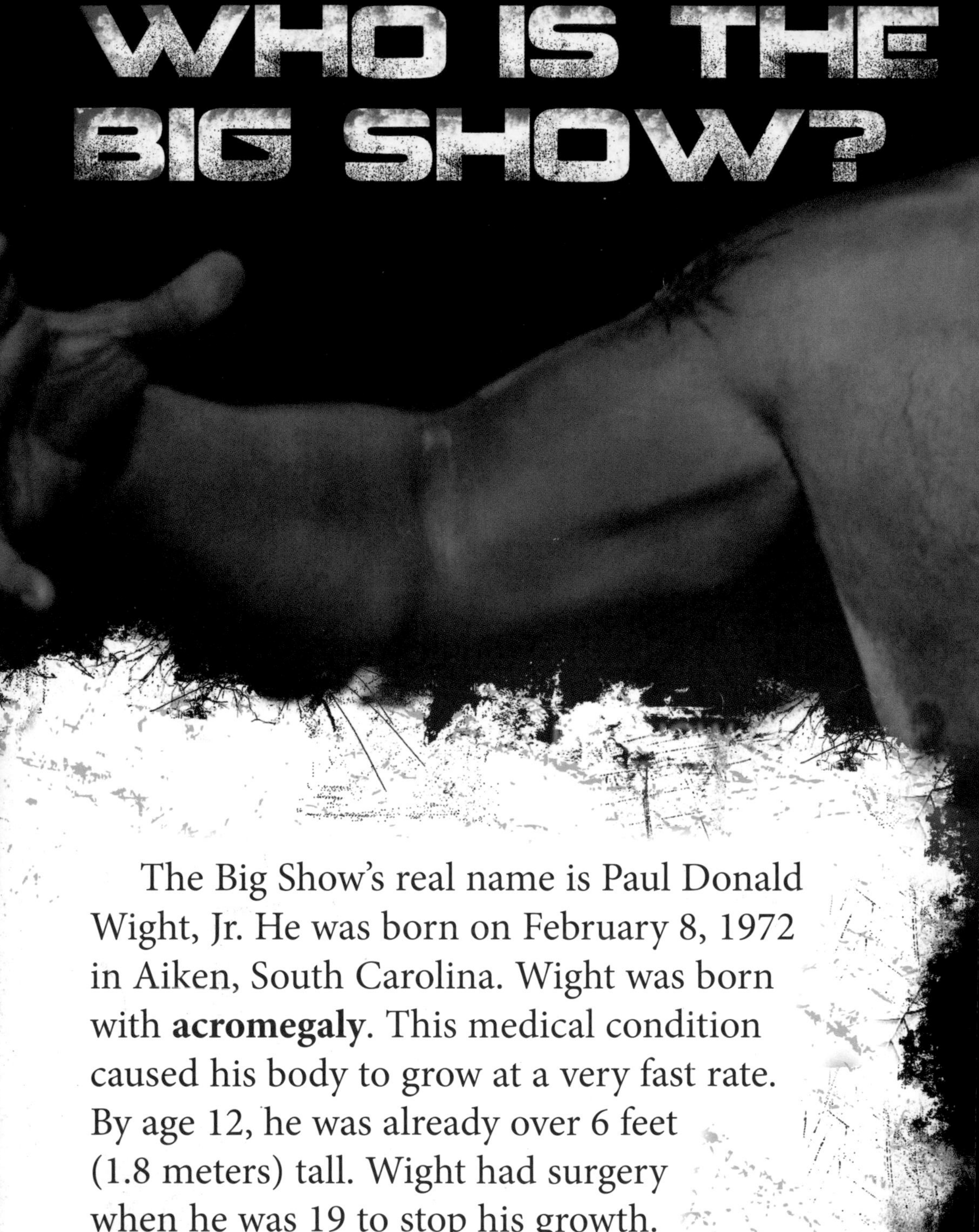

The Big Show's real name is Paul Donald Wight, Jr. He was born on February 8, 1972 in Aiken, South Carolina. Wight was born with **acromegaly**. This medical condition caused his body to grow at a very fast rate. By age 12, he was already over 6 feet (1.8 meters) tall. Wight had surgery when he was 19 to stop his growth.

Wight was a star athlete in high school. He played both football and basketball. After high school, Wight went to Wichita State University. He played as a **center** on the basketball team. Later, he moved to Southern Illinois University.

GO BIG

Wight's big break came when he met wrestler Hulk Hogan at a charity basketball event. Hogan told Wight that his size and strength would make him a great wrestler. Wight soon began to train. World Championship Wrestling (WCW) signed him to a contract in 1995. He first wrestled as The Giant.

BECOMING A CHAMPION

Wight first wrestled on television in June of 1995. He claimed to be the son of André the Giant. André suffered from acromegaly and died in 1993. Wight blamed Hogan for André's death. The two began a **feud**. Soon, Wight wrestled Hogan for the WCW Championship and won. At age 23, Wight became the youngest WCW Champion.

QUICK HIT!

Unlike Wight, André the Giant did not seek treatment for acromegaly. He was 7 feet, 5 inches (2.3 meters) tall and weighed 540 pounds (240 kilograms) when he died.

HULK
HOGAN

In 1999, Wight joined World Wrestling Entertainment (WWE). Wight was first called Big Nasty. Later, his name changed to The Big Show. Wight started as a **heel** in a group of wrestlers called The Corporation. He soon changed sides and became a **face** for The Union.

QUICK HIT!

The Big Show has had feuds with Brock Lesnar, The Rock, Steve Austin, Jack Swagger, and many other wrestling stars.

The Big Show has many **signature moves**. One is the bear hug. He wraps his huge arms around his opponent and squeezes as hard as he can. Another is the cobra clutch. The Big Show pins the opponent facedown on the mat and pulls his neck back.

The Big Show's **finishing move** is the powerful chokeslam. He grabs his opponent by the neck and lifts him off the ground. Then he slams the wrestler down to the mat. Few can stand their ground against the massive size and crushing force of The Big Show.

GLOSSARY

acromegaly—a medical condition that causes the body to grow very fast; people who have acromegaly never stop growing.

center—a basketball position that plays close to the hoop; centers are usually very tall.

chokeslam—a move in which a wrestler picks up his opponent by the neck and slams him down to the mat

face—a wrestler seen by fans as a hero

feud—a long-lasting conflict between two people or teams

finishing move—a wrestling move meant to finish off an opponent so that he can be pinned

heel—a wrestler seen by fans as a villain

rival—a competitor with whom one is in a heated feud

signature moves—moves that a wrestler is famous for performing

TO LEARN MORE

AT THE LIBRARY

Black, Jake. *The Ultimate Guide to WWE.* New York, N.Y.: Grosset & Dunlap, 2010.

Davies, Ross. *André the Giant.* New York, N.Y.: Rosen Pub. Group, 2001.

Price, Sean. *The Kids' Guide to Pro Wrestling.* Mankato, Minn.: Edge Books, 2012.

ON THE WEB

Learning more about The Big Show is as easy as 1, 2, 3.

1. Go to www.factsurfer.com.

2. Enter "The Big Show" into the search box.

3. Click the "Surf" button and you will see a list of related Web sites.

INDEX

The images in this book are reproduced through the courtesy of: WireImage / Getty Images, front cover, p. 17; Getty Images, pp. 4, 15 (small), 18-19; Zuffa LLC / Getty Images, p. 5; Titan Sports / Everett / Rex USA, p. 7; George Koroneos, pp. 8-9; Department of Defense, pp. 10-11; Rex / Rex USA, pp. 12, 14-15, 16; David Seto, pp. 13, 20-21.